Rewilding

Giving Nature a Second Chance

Dedicated to our parents, Kathleen and Henry Barnett, who took pleasure in the pathless woods—JD and AL

Cover art/design by Pixel Hive Studio
Edited by Catherine Marjoribanks
Designed by Pixel Hive Studio

Acknowledgments

We thank the following people for providing information and ideas central to the development of this book: Dr. Pete Ewins, Jon Hayes, Trevor Kinley, David Love, Gerald McKeating, and Dave Salmoni.

We particularly thank Dr. Art Weis for directing us to useful research and for his comments on our outline and early manuscript.

The following friends helped us track down photographs: Barb Cochrane, Jean and Jerry Oakes, and Sandrine De Ribaupierre.

We write with the full support of our wonderful families — and that makes our craft possible and efforts worthwhile!

Special thanks to our editor Catherine Marjoribanks and to RIck Wilks, Rivka Cranley, and their remarkable team at Annick Press.

Annick Press Ltd.

We acknowledge the support of the Canada Council for the Arts and the Ontario Arts Council, and the participation of the Government of Canada/la participation du gouvernement du Canada for our publishing activities.

Cataloging in Publication

Drake, Jane, author

     Rewilding : giving nature a second chance / Jane Drake and Ann Love.

Includes bibliographical references and index.

Issued in print and electronic formats.

ISBN 978-1-55451-962-0 (hardcover).--ISBN 978-1-55451-961-3 (softcover).--

ISBN 978-1-55451-963-7 (EPUB).--ISBN 978-1-55451-964-4 (PDF)

     1. Wildlife reintroduction--Juvenile literature. 2. Environmentalism-- Juvenile literature. I. Love, Ann, author II. Title.

QL83.4.D73 2017   j639.9   C2017-901702-0

                                        C2017-901703-9

Published in the U.S.A. by Annick Press (U.S.) Ltd.
Distributed in Canada by University of Toronto Press.
Distributed in the U.S.A. by Publishers Group West.

Printed in China

Visit us at: www.annickpress.com

Visit Jane Drake and Ann Love at: janedrake.ca

Rewilding

Giving Nature a Second Chance

Jane Drake
and
Ann Love

annick press
toronto + berkeley

Contents

1 INTRODUCTION

What Is Rewilding?

Once a city known for smog, London, England, has cleaned up its act and opened green spaces where wild deer now graze.

People make choices: we can pollute the air and crowd our roadways or we can keep our human spaces healthy and safer for animals and people too.

We can land a probe on a speeding comet or slip a spacecraft into orbit around Jupiter—but protecting the natural world here on Earth? That's a challenge. Species are going extinct and habitats are being destroyed by pollution, the clearing of forests, and climate change. Biologists and concerned citizens work hard to halt and reverse these trends. In a crisis like this, we need bold, super-sized thinking.

Rewilding is a big, new idea. "Rewilders" are stepping back and completely rethinking the relationship between people and our living Earth.

Rewilders want to restore habitats to their natural state, easing the damage done by humans. They want to recreate wild environments that will support native species and make room for animals to move freely across vast spaces. In this way, they believe, we can help our endangered species survive … and thrive! And in return, we will keep reaping the benefits nature has to offer: clean air, fresh water, fertile soil, and valuable natural resources.

Some wildlife species, such as badgers, can survive near people, even in large cities.

When important species disappear from a habitat, rewilders look for ways to bring them back. But that's not simple. Biologists debate what lived in a landscape when it was last truly wild. How far back do we turn the clock? To before the bulldozer? Before the ax and shovel? To ice age times? Can playing with nature trigger unintended surprises? Do we really want to bring dangerous creatures back to places where large numbers of people now live?

Left alone, nature will eventually bring everything into a new balance—you could call that nature rewilding itself. But even with help from us, these changes won't happen overnight. Today, rewilders apply new ideas to conservation projects, big and small. Read on to learn about attempts to release tigers, wolves, and bears into the wild; efforts to create a safe, friendly route for butterfly migration; and projects to bring wildlife back into city spaces. Finally, we look at where rewilding is heading in the future.

Back to the Wild

You sprint along a trail winding through tall bushes. What a day! Wild grasses and shrubs reach your ears and, above, the sky is clear and blue.

Ahead you hear a sudden, muffled cry, and a thump. You slow down and just miss stepping on a smear of wet blood. A dog-like animal with a scruffy tail bounds along the path ahead of you, a small rabbit dangling helplessly from its mouth. The creature pauses, locks eyes with you, and then dives into the undergrowth. That was no dog—it was a coyote!

Wild coyotes hunt their prey in many North American cities.

Hunger. Blood. Death. This is wild!

A few years ago, officials decided to let this large city park return to nature. They hand-pulled plants that had spread from nearby gardens and seeded native ones. No grass mowing, no pesticide use. They called it *rewilding*, and they said it probably wouldn't be long before wild animals moved back in. Well, they were right!

You hear a rustle in the tall grass. You glance uneasily over your shoulder. What could it be? What other animals lived here before people came along and built the city, pushing them out? Wolves? Bears?

Your heart beats so hard it pulses in your throat. But the park feels exciting now, more real, and beautiful. Maybe people can share this space with wildness after all!

Small carnivores, like this red fox hidden in tall grasses, can hunt and feed their growing families in urban areas.

Cores, Corridors, and Keystone Species

Scientists believe successful rewilding projects need three things: cores, corridors, and keystone species.

Cores

Every plant and animal needs a specific amount of space, food, and water to survive. A core is a stretch of land large enough to support all forms of life that would exist there naturally in the wild. Some creatures, like grizzly bears and tigers, need huge cores. That's a tall order in a world bustling with people.

Corridors

Corridors are routes that connect cores so wildlife can travel across built-up or unfriendly areas to find food and mates. Corridors don't have to be totally wild but they must be natural enough so that native animals—and plants—will use them.

Animals use overpasses as corridors to move safely from core to core.

Keystone Species

In building construction, the wedge-shaped block at the top of an arch, steadying and locking all the other blocks in place, is called the keystone. In biology, a keystone species is an animal or plant that, more than most, keeps its habitat or ecosystem in balance.

Top carnivores such as cougars and wolves are keystone species because their hunting prevents the population of prey animals from getting too large and crowding out others in the habitat.

Top herbivores such as elephants and beavers are also keystone species because their trampling and dam engineering can change the landscape.

And people are keystone species too. Keystone species affect their whole habitat, even parts they don't have direct contact with.

Rewilders have to work hard to keep these three elements—cores, corridors, and keystone species—in balance. That means they have to think carefully about relationships between habitats, wildlife, and people. And they have to adjust to unexpected circumstances, modify their plans, fail, and try again.

Rewilding is big, complex, risky, and exciting!

The cougar is a keystone carnivore that keeps deer numbers in check.

Herds of reindeer (top left) and African elephants (right) require vast core areas to find enough food to raise their families.

Wild Again

The American buffalo is an eco-engineer that tramples grasses and wallows on dry ground.

As successful keystone carnivores, leopards hunt on the grasslands, then drag their prey up trees to feed in safety.

A habitat is not fully rewilded unless the all-important keystone species—the ones that help keep the environment in balance—thrive there.

As we know, large carnivores are keystone species because they eat species further down the food web and keep their numbers in check. That may seem harsh, but it actually promotes coexistence among all the different species that share a habitat.

Large herbivores like horses and deer graze the land, keeping it from getting overgrown and containing the spread of wildfires. Larger herbivores, like elephants, trample trees and shrubs so that sunlight can reach the soil for seedlings to grow. Herbivores are also keystone species when they act as eco-engineers and change the landscape by their dam building or burrowing. Eco-engineers promote diversity in a habitat because they open up new homes and food sources for other plants and animals.

Of course, bees, hummingbirds, and other major pollinators are keystone species too, because many plants rely on them to reproduce. When a habitat's pollinators disappear or change, so do the plants that grow there and the creatures that need those plants for food or shelter.

But when it comes to rewilding a keystone species in its habitat, sometimes all our efforts fail. Rewilders want to know why, and what to do next.

Zoos can help protect and save endangered species from extinction, but can zoo animals ever be brought back to live in the wild?

And what about the creatures that have no habitat to return to—are they out of luck, or can they be rewilded into a totally new landscape?

This section looks at stories of why some significant and keystone species start to disappear, and what happens when people try to help them live in the wild again. Sometimes people's behavior has to change. It takes a lot of hard work, but even when our best efforts fail, we learn valuable lessons.

Honeybees provide a critical eco-service by fertilizing plants while collecting pollen for themselves.

A Second Chance for Trumpeter Swans: A Classic Success Story

A pair of swans circle high over a remote lake, zeroing in on their breeding site from the previous year. As they land with a splash, their wild calls echo, trumpeting their safe return.

There is a necklace of thousands, maybe millions, of small, shallow lakes and waterways across northern North America. The trumpeter swan, a keystone herbivore, once played a significant ecological role in these wetlands. Aerating lake and river bottoms with their bills and feet, these large waterfowl moved nutrients around, keeping the lakes healthy and ensuring a continuing food source for many creatures.

Last Call of the Trumpeter

Trumpeter swans were numerous when Europeans arrived in North America in the 1600s, but thousands were shot each year for their quills, feathers, skin, and fishy-tasting meat. By 1935, there were only about 70 known trumpeters left in the wild, and the species was nearly extinct. Hunting them was banned in the 1930s, but the swan numbers were slow to recover.

With close study, scientists learned the trumpeter's unique needs. The swans are shy and will abandon their young if people disturb their nests. They get lead poisoning when they swallow lost fishing gear. And the trumpeter competes for nesting habitat with the more aggressive mute swan.

SAVE OUR WILD LIFE

DEPARTMENT OF THE INTERIOR   NATIONAL PARK SERVICE BIOLOGICAL SURVEY   DEPARTMENT OF AGRICULTURE

Trumpeter Transplants

One effort to rewild trumpeter swans focused on relocating them to a new habitat. In the early 1980s, trumpeters nesting in the Grande Prairie region of Alberta were threatened by shrinking habitat and human encroachment—they needed a new home. The wetlands in Elk Island National Park was an obvious choice for rewilding, and because it was parkland, the swans would be protected there by law.

Biologists transplanted family groups in mid-summer when the parents were molting and the young hadn't fledged and so couldn't fly. When fall came, they migrated south as usual, and the following spring, the young returned to Elk Island. Park officials banned tourists from disturbing nesting swans, and over the next 30 years, the swan population steadily increased. Now the Elk Island flock is thriving and spreading out to wild spaces near the park.

Rewilding the trumpeter swans was a success, and what really helped was the fact that their natural habitat—the little lakes and wetlands—was there to provide a home for them.

This trio of cygnets survived because their nest was undisturbed by curious people.

Trumpeter swans often return to the same remote lake, year after year, before the ice melts in spring.

The Prairie Dog: Underdog or Wonder Dog?

Hold onto your hard hat, roll up your sleeves. Engineers at work! Wait ... these engineers are furry? Prairie dogs are rebuilding their town!

When some keystone species disappear, their habitat changes in important ways. Perhaps a food source disappears, or a new predator comes on the scene, or the landscape is altered so there is nowhere to shelter. If the keystone species return, though, they can sometimes actually help rewild their habitat. Consider the prairie dog.

Tens of thousands of prairie dog towns, made up of tunnels and mounds, once flourished on the North American plains.

A prairie dog spots an intruder and shrieks an alarm, warning its grassland neighbors.

Prairie dogs live in underground colonies called "towns" on western grasslands from Canada to Mexico. Prairie dogs are important prey for coyotes, badgers, and eagles, and they are just about the *only* prey of the endangered black-footed ferret.

But prairie dogs are more than food. They are eco-engineers whose tunnel systems loosen up the earth and channel rainwater. And the soil they spread around in mounds outside their holes, fertilized by their droppings, supports a rich variety of grasses and flowers, attracting pollinators and insects. Tiger salamanders and ferrets make their homes in abandoned prairie dog holes.

A town of prairie dogs acts like one enormous keystone herbivore, and when buffalo are reintroduced to prairie dog grasslands, they both thrive in an ancient coexistence. The prairie dogs clip grasses and spread the seeds, and the buffalo chew the grasses down so the prairie dogs can see their enemies. When prairie dogs spot outsiders, they help everybody by letting out shrieks that warn their wild neighborhood.

Contrary to popular belief, few grazing buffalo or cattle break their legs tripping into prairie dog holes.

When Europeans arrived in North America and began to use the land for farming and ranching, prairie dogs were seen as nothing more than a nuisance. Millions were exterminated and their towns destroyed.

When biologists in New Mexico wanted to restore grasslands that had been damaged by human use, they used prairie dogs to rewild the habitat. They reintroduced the keystone species and let the burrowing rodents get to work. In no time, soil improved, more grass and flower varieties grew, and other wildlife moved in.

With luck, rewilders will bring back more colonies of this busy keystone species and restore its wild grassland habitats.

The American Eel: Hatch Me If You Can

What keystone species looks like a snake and tears its prey apart by spinning it faster than a skater can twirl? That's the American eel!

American eels live in the lakes and rivers of North America that flow from the east coast into the Atlantic Ocean. In past times, the number of tons of American eels in Lake Ontario was greater than the weight of all the other fish added together. But now eel numbers are plummeting everywhere, and biologists say that losing this abundant and dominant predator is having an effect on predator–prey relationships all across eastern North America. They believe it's important to fully rewild our lake and river systems, but it all hinges on helping the American eel recover.

Don't Judge the Eel by Its Slimy Skin

American eels live amazing lives. They lay their eggs somewhere in the vast, warm, seaweedy Sargasso Sea east of Florida. Newborns drift toward shore and swim up rivers, where they grow into adults, as big as a meter (3 feet) long. Many years later, these adults return to the Sargasso Sea to lay their eggs.

American eels are crucial to the food chain both as predators of young fish and as prey to birds such as this great blue heron.

A Slippery Slope

Eels started disappearing because of overfishing, pollution, and barriers on rivers. Even though young eels can wriggle across land for short distances as they make their way upstream, they have trouble getting around dams. Adults swimming downstream can get sucked into a dam's hydroelectric turbine and be chopped to pieces.

To bring back American eels, officials put limits on the numbers caught, cleaned up the rivers and streams they swim in, and built eel-ways—water ladders that give these fish a safe path around river dams—but it still feels like a losing battle.

The next step for biologists would be to hatch American eel eggs and release the young safely into the rivers. That has been done successfully with Atlantic salmon, another keystone fish in the same waters. But biologists have never found exactly where in the Sargasso Sea American eels lay their eggs. Without eggs, they can't help the eels rewild.

Rewilding the American eel's home lakes and rivers may never be complete until biologists can figure out how to help this keystone species make a comeback.

In many places, fishers are allowed to bag immature eels for the luxury food market.

Marmots and Condors: Homeless

"Twenty-three animals are now officially rewilded and off the endangered species list." The applause dies down as the meeting absorbs the news, and the chair continues, "Hard work has paid off. A fine announcement to start our 2025 International Rewilding Conference. Now we will vote on our continued support of two more species: the marmot and the condor. It's up to you to decide if trying to save them is a realistic choice."

In past times, Vancouver Island marmots and California condors performed unique and important services that had big impacts on their habitats—the marmots as eco-engineers, the condors as super-scavengers. Today, however, there are very few marmots and condors left in the wild, and there's little wilderness left that would provide a suitable home for them. Does rewilding offer them any hope for the future?

Easy Prey

For over a century, Vancouver Island forests were heavily cut—and the population of wild Vancouver Island marmots steadily dropped. But marmots dig extensive, deep, underground burrows into mountaintop meadows above the forests—so why were they being affected so drastically by logging down the mountainsides?

Biologists captured most of the surviving marmots for breeding. They were careful to release them only in safe habitat where logging had stopped. But—darn—the marmot numbers kept falling. What was going on?

Biologists now think marmots confuse tree-cut slopes for their treeless meadow homes. Young marmots mistakenly move into cut zones, where wolves and eagles easily ambush them. Climate change is another factor. Marmots hibernate, but they are likely to die during cold, windy winters because the insulating snow cover they need to blanket their burrows is thinner and melts sooner.

A Vancouver Island marmot freezes at the mouth of its burrow to avoid the attention of predators.

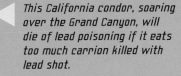

This California condor, soaring over the Grand Canyon, will die of lead poisoning if it eats too much carrion killed with lead shot.

The Not-So-Wild West

Thousands of years ago, when mammoths and giant camels roamed the American West, huge California condors scavenged the dead megabeasts for their meals. After these species became extinct, the condors survived on buffalo carcasses and beached sea mammals. But in the twentieth century, condor numbers crashed with the disappearance of the buffalo, along with habitat loss, poaching, and poisoning, both deliberate and accidental.

In 1987, conservation officers captured all 22 remaining condors and new legal protections were put in place. Condors lay one egg every two years, but they will lay a second if the first is taken. Breeders learned to raise the first in what they nicknamed a "condorminium" and let the parents rear the second. Soon, captive-bred condors were released into the wild, and by 2014, their numbers had climbed back up to more than 400. But without wild buffalo herds—surprise—they have to be fed. Officers place dead cows near condor nests. It's not clear whether the West will ever be wild enough for this scavenger to survive on its own.

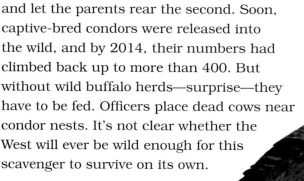

California condors were reintroduced into Arizona and Mexico, as well as California.

Are They Worth It?

The fate of the Vancouver Island marmots and the condors raises an important question for conservationists. Should we continue to support endangered species even if they have no home to return to, or would it be better to direct our efforts and money to rewilding species whose habitats can successfully support them?

Since 2003, conservationists have released hundreds of captive-bred marmots back into the wild.

People donate to save the cute and cuddly-looking marmot— but is that possible?

Zoos: Keepers of Endangered Species

Your eyes lock with the pacing predator's. You've watched it bang the gate and scuff the dirt with its paws. Your gut tells you to open the cage and let it free. But where would it go? Is a zoo the only choice for this magnificent wild creature?

Breeding programs in zoos provide genetic lifeboats for endangered species such as this lion (right) and gorilla (above).

If rewilding is defined as species living free and on their own in the wild, what role, exactly, do zoos play?

All wild species and spaces are challenged by habitat loss and competition from other creatures, including people. Many species become endangered or locally extinct (entirely gone in one area, though still existing elsewhere). When natural core habitats are gone or severely limited, there is no room in the wild for more breeding pairs. At this point, those animals living and reproducing in zoos are the only hope for future generations. And when a species' numbers drop below a sustainable level—the number of animals needed for a healthy population—zoos may be their only chance for *future* rewilding in a safe core that may exist some day.

Building a Genetic Lifeboat

Some endangered species—pygmy hogs, dart frogs, Arabian oryx—have been kept alive by captive breeding programs in zoos around the world. When their numbers in the wild drop very low, zoologists use captive animals to create a so-called genetic lifeboat, preserving enough creatures to keep the species from going extinct.

The Arabian oryx, an antelope from the deserts of the Middle East, was hunted for food, as a trophy, and to be kept as an exotic pet. By 1972, the oryx was extinct in the wild and found only with private collectors and in zoos.

The Phoenix Zoo in Arizona took action and began a breeding program using their own animals and males and females from other zoos. The Arabian oryx was gradually reintroduced and has now been successfully rewilded in its former range, with numbers now topping a thousand, with thousands more in zoos.

Giving from the Grave

Zoologists routinely collect reproductive specimens from critically endangered species. For instance, frozen sperm from a now-dead tiger can help a living female tiger reproduce.

Once near extinction, the incredible oryx finds food in the desert.

Zoo Tigers: Back to the Wild

The young biologist accelerates his pickup truck along a dusty track. An upright stuffed antelope is tied on behind, its hooves sliding along the ground. Nearby, two collared tigers stand puzzled for a moment—and then give chase.

Tigers are magnificent keystone carnivores, but they don't make ideal neighbors because they will eat people. In the animal's Asian homelands, farmers continue to expand into tiger territory—and both humans and tigers die as a result. As few as 3,000 tigers still survive in the wild. Meanwhile, tens of thousands live in captivity around the world—about 3,000 in Texas alone—mostly as exotic pets.

Biologists would like to support the wild tiger population, but they need to find new core habitats away from human population. And many think it makes sense to prepare some of the captive zoo and pet tigers for release into the wild.

In 2000, a bold tiger experiment began in South Africa on a grassland reserve, Tiger Canyons. Tigers are not native to Africa, but the plan was to teach captive tigers to survive in the wild there and then bring them back to their homeland in Asia when enough suitable tiger habitat became available. Enter zoologist Dave Salmoni with two zoo-born tigers, Ron and Julie. His job: teach these seven-month-old, leash-trained cubs to hunt.

For three years, Salmoni worked with the cubs as they practiced spotting, stalking, ambushing, and eating African wild prey. Yes, eating—one of the hardest lessons for the cubs to learn was that prey is dinner.

At first Salmoni taught them to chase down dead animals pulled behind a truck. Hungry, Ron and Julie eventually fed on warthog, ostrich, springbok, and other African antelopes as large as wildebeest.

There are more pet tigers than wild tigers in the world— can we teach them to hunt and set them free?

A Bengal tiger surveys Tiger Canyons, South Africa, from the roof of a safari truck.

Over a dozen cubs have been born at Tiger Canyons, but plans to move the offspring to Asia fell through. Finding enough available habitat for them was still a problem. And Ron and Julie were a mix of zoo tiger subspecies, so some scientists believed it would be a bad idea to introduce to Asia tigers that were not purebred.

Ron and Julie and their offspring stayed in South Africa, and today the population lives on their own kills. While raising animals outside their own native habitat is not ideal, this rewilding strategy, known as translocation, is one way to help keep a keystone species alive. Meanwhile, in Asia, conservationists aim to double the tiger population by securing more wild core habitats for tigers—as far away from people as possible.

If more core habitats become available in their native Asia, scientists hope tigers will thrive again.

Getting It Right

This humpback whale needs oceans of water to survive in the wild.

People who live in high-rises need green spaces to restore their bodies and spirits.

Every plant and animal needs a certain amount of core space to thrive. That space has to include the right arrangement of water, food, and shelter for the species. A whale needs a lot more water than, say, a shrimp. In rewilding, a core is a stretch of habitat large enough to support all the forms of life that exist there naturally in the wild.

How big does a core need to be? A wolf pack needs anywhere from 250 to 2,500 square kilometers (100 to 1,000 square miles) of territory, the size of 50,000 to 500,000 football fields; deer have a home range of 2 to 20 square kilometers (1 to 8 square miles), the size of 400 to 4000 football fields; elephants need between 10 and 70 square kilometers (4 to 27 square miles), bigger than the size of Manhattan, unless they have to migrate greater distances for water.

A deer herd this large needs a vast area of woodland edge and meadow to thrive without chewing down or destroying all the plants.

Do people belong in cores? People have their own place in the natural web of life, and cores usually contain natural resources that people need—trees, minerals, water, and good soil for crops. But rewilding can be a huge challenge if people pollute the air, water, and soil; dam the rivers; clear-cut the forests; and build roads and communities. So, depending on how we behave, people can often create the biggest challenges for rewilding. And sometimes, when large carnivores are around, rewilding creates big challenges for people too.

Wolf Country Again: Yellowstone National Park

"Ooooooooooo," howls the wolf: jaws open, green eyes narrowed. She lowers her head and sniffs. "Ahoooooooo," she calls again. Swiveling her ears, she hears her own echo, and then silence.

Wolf Free

Wolves are a wilderness species. They live in closely knit groups called packs. Each pack has a leader—an alpha male or breeding female—and an extended family. They hunt, travel, raise pups, and mark and guard their territory as a team. Aside from humans, wolves are the top keystone predator wherever they live—unless they meet a wild tiger.

In 1872, Yellowstone National Park became the first national park anywhere in the world. A vast wilderness, it is located in the northwest corner of Wyoming, and it looks like a puzzle piece, with its borders touching Montana and Idaho. Unlike parks of today, protecting wildlife was not its main purpose. The systematic elimination of wild predators was government policy throughout the United States, and by 1926, the last pair of gray wolves in the park was dead. Yellowstone was wolf-free.

Scientists know wolves form strong family bonds and are loyal to their leader.

Wolves have had bad press for hundreds of years.

Good Riddance

Wolves have a long history of being feared, even hated. In medieval Europe, the Roman Catholic Church declared that the wolf was the devil's dog. In folklore, wolves were bloodthirsty villains. To American settlers, ranchers, and ordinary citizens, wolves were pests. They competed with people for game meat, threatened livestock, and were thought to be a danger to small children. Governments offered bounties for their pelts. By 1930, wolves were gone from most states.

Yellowstone Without Wolves

With the wolves gone, elk, their favorite prey, increased in population, overgrazed the grasses, and feasted on young saplings. Herds gathered by rivers, drinking and uprooting the plants that held the banks. Soil fell in and clouded the water, changing the habitat for fish and other aquatic life. Without enough trees, grasses, and seeds, songbirds moved on and the beaver population was reduced to one dam. Coyotes, accustomed to freeloading off the remains of wolf kills, adapted their diets and preyed on small game. Without wolves, the ecosystem was out of balance.

Wolves howl to communicate with their family group and other packs.

Release the Wolves

The blades of the helicopter slice through the cold Alberta sky as the pilot zooms in. Steady, aim, and *whoosh*. The tranquilizing dart hits the mark. It doesn't take long to land the chopper and track down the sleeping wolf. Her travel crate is waiting.

In 1974, the United States declared wolves an endangered species. This helped change the way people thought about them—as animals to be protected, not feared—and gave a boost to those planning for their return to their old habitat. Wild wolves from Canada were eventually selected for release into Yellowstone National Park. Those chosen for monitoring were fitted with radio-collars.

Some people tried blocking the release program with protests and legal action, fearing wolves would kill livestock, and maybe children too. But in March 1995, 14 wolves were set free in Yellowstone, with 17 added the following year.

The wolves hit the ground running, dividing into packs, each of which established its own territory. As a core territory, the national park still had everything they needed to thrive, and it offered all the room they needed to roam. With plentiful prey, the wolves successfully raised many pups. By the year 2000, they numbered about 120. The wolf was once again Yellowstone's top dog!

For a successful hunt, wolves must work as a team to separate the weak and the young from a large buffalo herd.

From the Top Down

Most believe that the wolf has brought Yellowstone National Park back into balance. Scientists judge this by watching the *trophic cascade*—a phenomenon in which the top predator, even though it kills its prey, has a positive impact on the entire ecosystem.

Elk herds shrank and the survivors moved to higher ground, where wolves had to work harder to catch them. Coyote numbers fell, while fox and rodent numbers rose. Scavengers such as bears, foxes, eagles, hawks, ravens, crows, patient coyotes, and insects all benefited from the wolves' leftovers.

With wolves keeping elk in check, young trees began to take hold along riverbanks. Sapling cottonwood and willow now provide shade for spawning fish, homes for songbirds, shelter for pronghorn antelope, and food for beavers. The verdict is in: Yellowstone has been successfully rewilded.

Beyond the Yellowstone Core

Wolves are protected within the core habitat of Yellowstone. Beyond the borders, it's a different story.

Individual states control which species are designated as endangered. When wolf numbers increased, Wyoming took wolves off the endangered species list. Hunters killed more than half of the non-park wolf population in less than a year.

The wolf faces hostility in ranching communities outside the park. Government and nonprofit organizations pay ranchers when they can prove wolves killed their livestock, but some ranchers take action on their own, with the motto "Shoot, shovel, and shut up."

A wolf can wolf down 10 kilograms (22 pounds) of meat in one meal.

Namibia: Conservation at Its Core

Prey and predators collide, grunt, and growl. A high-pitched scream sears the air. The gruesome sounds of tearing flesh, crunching on bones, and snarling stop. Heavy paws draw closer, crushing dry leaves, then the lion flops down beside the tent, a few feet from the tourists' heads.

Lions hunt and feed at night, then snooze and sleep by day.

Cores from Nothing

The name Namibia means "vast space" or "nothingness." For a century, Namibia was ruled by colonial powers who took a reckless approach to rules concerning hunting and poaching. By the time the country achieved its independence in 1990, the damage was done: 80 percent of its wildlife had disappeared. The new democratic government hoped to turn things around by making protection of the natural environment a priority, giving rights to wildlife under the constitution, and setting aside almost half of the land for its wild "citizens." Almost the whole country was rewilded.

Working Together

Namibia is now divided into conservancies—large core habitats where wildlife is protected. People share the land with lions, leopards, elephants, and rhinos because the country's wildlife brings in tourists, and tourism is crucial to the country's economy. Animals mean jobs, money for schools, and better health care.

Where hunting is illegal, neighbors are vigilant about turning in poachers. Namibia, unlike nearby countries, has a growing wildlife population, and more free-ranging cheetahs than anywhere else.

How do Namibians solve conflicts between wildlife and people? They get creative. For example, lions hunt at night and will go wherever they see prey. So to make their domestic animals harder to spot, farmers use screening on fences and keep trained dogs to warn when lions are near. Elephants will sniff out communal water tanks and end up destroying them when they come for a drink, but smudge-pot fires sprinkled with hot peppers keep elephants trekking to the next water hole.

Rewilding Revolutionaries

Namibia has led the way in Africa, providing significant core space for the rewilding of wildlife species. The country's success with ecotourism demonstrates the benefits of living in balance with nature. Now neighboring countries look to Namibia and its citizens to learn how people can live in harmony with wildlife. It's a win-win situation!

Ecotourists gather at a Namibian water hole to snap photos of springbok and zebra.

Europe: Green at Heart

At two years old, a bear leaves the forest where he was born. The instinct to find new territory, far from his mother's den, is strong. What does he know, or care, about international borders?

On May 22, 2006, German news headlines screamed: FIRST SIGHTING IN 170 YEARS: WILD BEAR CAUSES CHAOS IN BAVARIA.

This bear, known officially as JJ1, had been born to a pair of brown bears that were part of a recent rewilding project bringing bears back to the Italian Alps.

After the bear crossed their border, German reporters nicknamed him Bruno, and headlines declared: IN BAVARIA WE WELCOME BEARS. But after Bruno killed 33 sheep, 4 rabbits, some hens, some goats, and a guinea pig, he got another name: Problem Bear. When officers couldn't catch Bruno, they shot him on June 26.

Bruno or JJ1, aka Problem Bear, now stands stuffed in the Munich Museum.

Young male bears naturally wander great distances. The core area in Italy where Bruno and his parents lived may not have been large enough for successful bear rewilding, and Bruno didn't understand about borders. He didn't know that farm animals aren't supposed to be bear food. People panicked when he broke their rules.

Blood in Transylvania

Transylvania, Romania, is wilder than Bavaria, with a huge core of mountain forests. The last Romanian dictator decreed hunting off limits to everyone but himself. When he was overthrown in 1989, plenty of bear, wolf, and lynx still stalked the Transylvanian mountains. Romanians felt lucky to have so much wildlife. Forest cores in other European countries had long since lost most or all of their keystone carnivores to hunters.

Starting in 1993, Romanian biologists educated townspeople, shepherds, and farmers on how to live safely near cores and carnivores, and encouraged them to do so. This meant cleaning up garbage, electrifying fences, and training guard dogs. Romania's Carpathian Large Carnivore Project helped set up the Piatra Craiului National Park, a protected wildlife reserve promoting biodiversity, in 1999.

In 2014, rewilders released a small herd of European bison near Piatra Craiului. The core seemed perfect for these rare keystone herbivores. But the bison were attacked by a pack of 15 stray dogs. Four died, including the first calf born in the wild. Further research revealed that Romania has thousands of stray dogs that threaten not only bison but also the food supply of native wolves. It reminds us that rewilding is complicated, with many different—and sometimes unexpected—factors that can get in the way of success.

With their snowshoe-like paws, lynx hunt with ease on top of the snow. ▶

The Newfoundland and Labrador Cod Fishery: Come and Gone and Back Again

In about 1000 CE, Viking explorers encountered cod off the coast of Newfoundland. Five hundred years later, John Cabot reported, "The sea is covered with fish which are caught not merely with nets but with baskets." And another five hundred years later? These early explorers would not believe what happened next.

Word of Cabot's find turned cod into a hot trading commodity. Ships from Europe arrived each summer carrying salt for preserving fish, and they sailed back home in the fall with salted cod. From the mid-1600s onwards, settlers made cod fishing their life, and small communities sprang up along the coasts.

Cod, a keystone species, is needed to keep crustaceans and smaller fish populations in check. They prefer shallow water, so the coast was their core habitat, as well as the Grand Banks—underwater plateaus where cold and warm water currents meet.

Young cod numbers are finally on the rise.

Technology and Greed

Until the 1970s, the supply of fish seemed to keep pace with the growth of the fishing industry. But then came bigger, better boats. Trawlers, equipped with weighted nets, dragged the ocean floor, taking cod of all sizes as well as "incidental catch"—unwanted fish and marine life snared along the way.

Radar, sonar, and aircraft helped track down the remaining cod core habitats. Canadian fishers had generous quotas, and foreign trawlers and factory ships took huge numbers of cod as well. When cod stocks fell, the cod's main food—capelin and shrimp—started eating cod eggs. This role reversal—prey eating its predator—contributed to the cod's decline. Soon, the cod numbers fell disastrously.

Cod fishing had been an integral part of industry in Newfoundland and Labrador for many centuries.

The minister of fisheries, a Newfoundlander, closed Canadian waters to cod fishing in July 1992. Overnight, 30,000 people were out of work and a way of life ground to a halt.

It didn't have to happen that way. Newfoundlanders had warned government authorities that cod numbers were dwindling, but not enough was done to keep out foreign fishers.

In the spring of 2016, one core area in southern Newfoundland reopened to sustainable cod fishing—a hopeful sign. Left alone, the sea had rewilded itself. Now, given a second opportunity, Canadian fishers and their government have a chance to prove that they can be good stewards of the environment.

▼ Before electricity and refrigeration, the people from Newfoundland and Labrador ate and exported salted cod.

Core Values: A Wild Ride in the Netherlands

You're a wild horse living on lush, natural grasslands with no predators—could life be any better? But what happens when there are more and more horses and not enough food to go around?

In 1968 in the Netherlands, Dutch farmers drained a stretch of inland sea the size of Manhattan and, by chance, never used the reclaimed land. Over time, a big marsh formed at one end, attracting rare long-legged wetland birds such as spoonbills, egrets, and bitterns as well as the stately greylag goose and white-tailed eagle. The Dutch named the place Oostvaardersplassen, "wetlands to the east."

Politicians want hotels built overlooking the park so tourists can view the Konik ponies.

Ancestor of the domestic goose, the greylag has returned to the restored wild marshes of Oostvaardersplassen.

Meanwhile, on higher ground, saplings rooted and a forest started growing into the wetland. The Dutch have almost no wild marsh left and Oostvaardersplassen was a new-found treasure. What to do?

The forest service decided to introduce large herbivores to trample the saplings and encourage wild grasses. Their herbivore choices included red deer from Scotland, Konik ponies, and Heck cattle. The last two are ancient breeds, thought to be close relatives to the extinct tarpan and aurochs, forebears of our domestic horse and cow. Deer, tarpan, and aurochs likely grazed nearby during the ice age.

Red deer face challenges finding food where the land is overbrowsed.

No predators were introduced to keep their population in check, so when the herbivores were let free into the core, they grew in number until there were too many for the core to support.

Then, each winter, four of every ten herbivores would die of exposure and starvation. Outraged animal rights activists insisted the government shoot weak animals out of mercy. The idea of introducing wolves was dismissed—Oostvaardersplassen is too close to farms and towns. The best solution the government could find was to assemble land to allow the herbivores to travel outside the core when food and shelter run short.

Some call Oostvaardersplassen a cruel experiment. Others call it a sensational example of rewilding. In fact, it's a work in progress—a human-built core with humans acting as the only keystone species keeping wildlife in balance. So far, corridors linking that core to others are incomplete. But for most of the Dutch, who live in a small country with millions of people, intense farming, and manufacturing, Oostvaardersplassen offers a breath of magnificent wild nature—free, refreshing, and exciting.

Natural Connections

This wild elephant does not want to share his traditional path with travelers on a Sri Lankan road.

Tourist adventurers visit Mt. Everest every year.

We live in a global, connected world. Information travels instantly, and people are mobile like never before. Adventurers invade the most inhospitable places, such as Mt. Everest and the South Pole. The more we humans spread out over Earth, the less space we leave for wilderness. Keystone species that once roamed freely across vast regions, never encountering humans, are now often hemmed into increasingly restricted core habitats. And if they venture out, they can wander into conflict and danger.

Whether they are migrating, traveling in search of food or mates, or fleeing from enemies, keystone species often cross from one core to another. What they need, then, are corridors that safely link these parts of their habitat. Without safe corridors, these species face hazards presented by farms, roads, and cities. And when large predators and humans come face-to-face, trouble can follow.

Some communities have met this challenge head-on with creative solutions. But it's not necessarily straightforward. For instance, international borders mean nothing to wildlife. And we might have to learn to respect the corridors that the animals have chosen, whether or not they are convenient for us.

Conservationists hope that collisions between animals and people will be reduced by strategic wildlife bridges over highways.

Over and Under: Wildlife Corridors in Banff National Park

"Why did the grizzly cross the road?"

"To get to the other side!"

People who live in busy cities know that getting around can be hazardous. So we have stoplights, crosswalks, sidewalks, and other safety measures to make sure that everyone's journey is safe and respected. Compared to a lot of animal species, we've got it good!

A Walk in the Park

In March 2017, hikers spotted grizzly bear 122, fresh from his den in Banff National Park. After hibernating for over six months, he was hungry and cranky. Park officials posted alerts warning people to carry bear spray, keep dogs on leashes, and watch for signs of bear.

Wildlife crossing over a highway in Banff National Park, Canada. ▶

Like you, grizzlies move around their territory. But big carnivores must travel vast distances to find food, mates, and dens while avoiding people and especially their multilane highways. Bear 122, one of about 80 in the park, may wander over 4,000 square kilometers (1,544 square miles) in the coming months and never step on pavement. But if he crosses a road, he risks his life.

The Trans-Canada Highway runs the width of Banff National Park, and when it expanded to four lanes, park authorities set out to reduce the number of road-killed animals. First, they installed fencing, which keeps many animals off the highway. Next, they constructed animal crossovers—six bridges over and 38 tunnels under the road.

Deer took to the crossovers immediately, followed by cougars, wolves, lynx, wolverines, snakes, and even toads. Grizzlies were nervous at first, but now officials believe mother bears teach their young to use the wildlife corridors.

Banff National Park has nearly four million visitors annually, mostly in the summer months when wildlife is active. As a successful rewilding project, the crossover corridors allow creatures like bear 122 to stay wild while people drive through one of the most spectacular landscapes in the world.

These bighorn sheep are leaping onto the highway, endangering themselves and tourists driving past.

Australia: Reduce, Reuse, Recycle ... and Rewild?

You have scrap sheet metal, used lumber, and—for tools—a saw, shovel, hammer, and nails. Your challenge: construct reptile hideaways. And make them safe to step on.

Students from Australia's Jerramungup District High School met the challenge and turned an abandoned sheep farm into a section of wildlife corridor linking core habitats. The aim was to involve the students in the rewilding project and, at the same time, turn damaged land into better habitat for reptiles. Instead of chopping down any of the scarce trees for materials, organizers supplied the kids with recycled pieces from old sheds to build the reptile shelters. As the students worked, they discovered rare skinks, geckos, and snakes never before recorded on the site.

Students use recycled planks to make reptile hideaways.

Alien Invaders

In the last 200 years, many unique reptiles, birds, and mammals have disappeared from Australia. The cause? People.

Early European settlers introduced foxes, house cats, and rabbits—none of which have natural predators in Australia. These new species spread rapidly across the country, edging out native animals.

European farmers also cleared bushland for farming. With native plants bulldozed or plowed under, the sun sucked water out of the soil, leaving a salty crust after only a few years. In many places, their non–native European crops withered, pasture grew scarce for domestic sheep, and foreign weeds invaded.

Faced with both damaged land and wildlife extinction, Australians are turning to rewilding. The corridor that the students were working on is part of the Gondwana Link, a 1,000-kilometer (620-mile) plan to connect southwest national park cores. The vision calls for—when possible—the rewilding of unusually wide corridors between the cores so that, over time, some of the corridor lands will also become core. The farm rewilded by the students is already a lifeline for reptiles as well as the marvelous black-gloved wallaby, honey possum, and cockatoo.

Honey possums like to feast on the blossom of the strange Banksia plant.

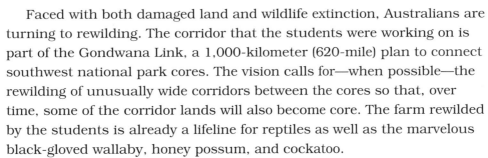

The black-gloved wallaby has a fighting chance if part of the corridor in Gondwana Link is completed.

Butterfly Corridors: Linking Canada, the United States, and Mexico

A flash of orange and black flits by—a monarch butterfly, traveling with a purpose. Born in early fall on a milkweed plant in southern Canada, it migrates to Mexico. There, it hibernates in a remote forest with millions of other monarchs, saving energy for the return flight. But this elderly insect will only fly as far as Texas. There, it will find a milkweed plant, lay eggs, fold its tattered wings, and die. Two more generations of monarchs will travel north through the United States, laying eggs on milkweed and dying before the journey to Canada is complete.

Nature made life complicated for monarchs, but for countless generations, they flourished. Twenty years ago, however, their numbers began to decline dramatically, and by 2013, with their habitats under siege, the monarchs were close to extinction.

The Fall of the Monarch

Adult monarch butterflies drink nectar from many plants, but their favorites are routinely sprayed with deadly pesticides. Monarch caterpillars eat only milkweed leaves, but farmers and roadside workers often pull this plant, calling it a "noxious weed." Climate change—storms, strong winds, and changing temperatures—kills butterflies. The small forests where monarchs shelter in winter are being illegally logged, reducing available habitat.

The Monarch Rules Again

Pollinators play a crucial role in the life of plants that people and animals need for survival. In a national project to protect pollinators, the U.S. government is building a unique wildlife corridor. Plans include planting millions of milkweed and other nectar-rich plants along either side of the Interstate 35 Highway that runs right down the middle of the country, from Duluth, Minnesota, to Laredo, Texas. The plants will provide food and breeding sites for migrating butterflies. Bees and bats—also keystone pollinators—will benefit from this corridor, as will birds and a variety of insects.

Changing the laws about noxious weeds can make a difference too. For example, Toronto now welcomes milkweed and encourages people to plant it. A patchwork milkweed corridor helps the butterflies move through the big city. And "Milkweed Madness" has struck the state of Ohio. Citizens are planting local milkweed varieties, helping to extend the I-35 corridor. Plus, the monarch's winter home in Mexico is now protected in a huge nature reserve.

Monarch caterpillars only eat milkweed leaves.

Jaguar Ground-Truthing: Corridors in Costa Rica

A motion-sensitive camera captures an animal crossing a riverbank trail. A field biologist checks out the photo and stares into the flashing eyes of a jaguar. Massive head. Glistening fangs. Distinctive black rosettes on its flank. Next frame—the cat is almost out of range. Usually this keystone carnivore runs so fast after the first flash, there is no second photo! Now here is proof that jaguars use this exact brushy patch as a corridor between cores.

Hounded from New Mexico to Argentina

Ancient Central and South American cultures such as the Aztec, Maya, and Inca revered the jaguar as a master spirit, a figure of power and strength. But when Europeans took over the lands for ranching, the newcomers assumed that jaguars ate cattle and so they hunted them down. Later, people started to shoot jaguars for trophy heads and fur coats. Eventually, the surviving jaguars took cover in remote core hideouts. Jaguars were declared a threatened species.

When biologists were able to prove that most jaguars do not kill cattle, preferring wild prey, the tide of opinion began to turn. By 1980, hunting this magnificent keystone species was ruled illegal in most countries, as was transporting trophy heads and skins across borders.

A Mayan god looks fierce with its jaguar headdress.

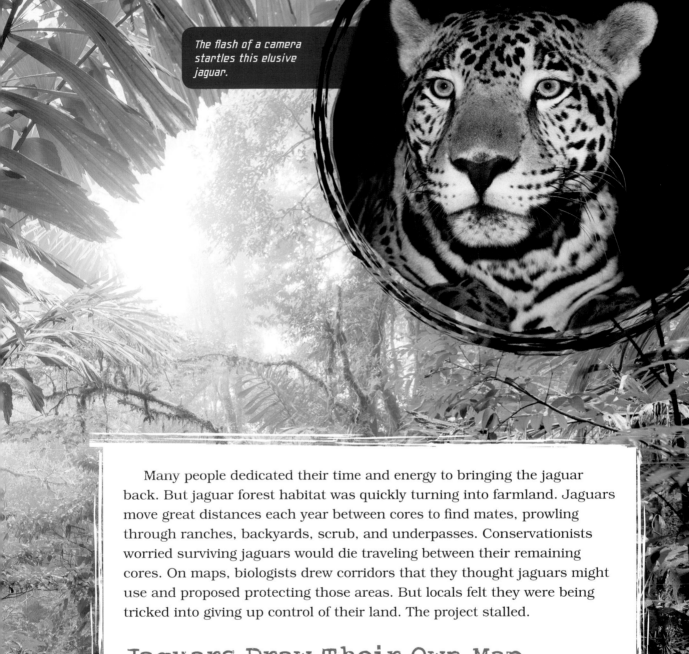

The flash of a camera startles this elusive jaguar.

Many people dedicated their time and energy to bringing the jaguar back. But jaguar forest habitat was quickly turning into farmland. Jaguars move great distances each year between cores to find mates, prowling through ranches, backyards, scrub, and underpasses. Conservationists worried surviving jaguars would die traveling between their remaining cores. On maps, biologists drew corridors that they thought jaguars might use and proposed protecting those areas. But locals felt they were being tricked into giving up control of their land. The project stalled.

Jaguars Draw Their Own Map

Then Alan Rabinowitz, an American biologist, and his team decided to collect local stories of sightings and kills, plus poop, paw prints, and photographs—a strategy called ground-truthing—to find the corridors jaguars actually use. If a corridor is ground-truthed, local landowners and their governments are more likely to help protect the pathway called *Paseo del Jaguar*. It's working in Costa Rica, and hopefully other nations that are home to jaguars will follow that country's lead.

Panda Bear: Bamboo or Bust

A male panda bear wanders into view, unaware that people are watching. Swaying his head, checking for intruders, he's scenting his territory. At one tree, he rubs the worn trunk with his head, neck, and body. Then he turns and adds a waxy substance from a scent gland in his bottom to the tree. Farther along, the bear backs up against a trunk and climbs the tree, backwards. Up he goes until his body is stretched out as far as possible. He lifts one leg and releases a torrent of urine that flies in every direction. This panda's saying, "I'm here. This is MY home. Back off!"

Once he has established his territory, this panda concentrates on eating bamboo.

In 1970, there were only 1,000 giant pandas left in the wilds of China. Human activities, including farming, forestry, and settlement, had shrunk panda habitat. Stranded on hilltops, these secretive, solitary creatures could not find mates. And biology worked against them. Their primary food—99 percent of their diet—is bamboo. Every five to fifteen years, different stands of bamboo trees suddenly bloom and die, eliminating a food source. Scientists found that when this happened, the bears were too nervous to pass through human territory in search of new stands of bamboo, and pandas starved.

A baby panda sleeps peacefully in an incubator: another success of China's breeding program.

The panda has become the international symbol of conservation. Through research and action, the World Wildlife Fund, together with the Chinese government, has saved this species from extinction. A captive breeding program boosted the bears' numbers, and reserves were set aside as development-free panda zones. Now corridors connecting the panda's domains are slowly being set up. When the corridors are planted with bamboo, pandas will at last be able to move safely from one core to another—grazing along the way.

5 Rewilding the Human World

The crowded urban landscape of New York City is seen from Central Park.

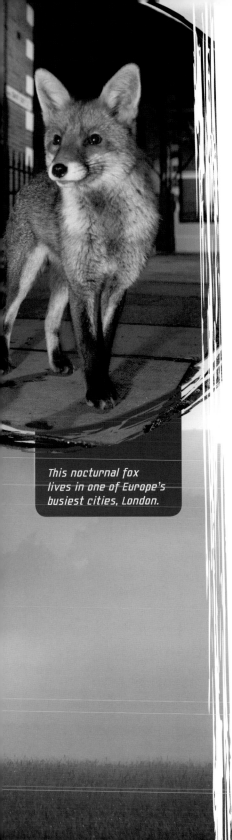

This nocturnal fox lives in one of Europe's busiest cities, London.

A little rewilding is better than none, and it can add a breath of fresh air to a crowded urban environment. This section focuses on city cores—a wall, a mining pit, a rooftop—small patches of rewilded cityscape.

City rewilding can create a hodgepodge habitat—a patchwork of space that provides little more than the necessary eco-services for species survival: food, space, and shelter. Sometimes in cities you'll discover that species have rewilded themselves. Nature takes hold, with or without our invitation. Plants and insects make their homes in empty lots or other green spaces and hold firm while neighborhoods expand around them. Animals move in as unlikely neighbors and find ways to coexist peacefully with city-dwellers.

Problems can arise when humans and wild animals don't agree about who is in charge. Some wild animals—like squirrels and raccoons—are especially good at adapting to an urban setting: we call them super-survivors. A raccoon that moves into your attic is a pest, but not a very threatening one. Now, sharing space with a top predator like a leopard—that really puts rewilding to the test!

For this American robin, an air duct is as good a nesting site as a tree branch.

City Sites:
Every Little Space Counts

A figure slips out of an alley into a vacant lot. It's dark, but you can see he wears gloves and cradles a small package in his hands. Crouching down, he looks side to side, then quietly digs, places the package in the hole, and creeps on.

A few months later, sprays of yellow wildflowers nod where the hole was dug. The plants are healthy, attracting keystone pollinators: wild bees and a hummingbird. The guerrilla gardener strikes again!

Civic engineers and architects are channeling nature too. More and more, they build structures with rewilding in mind—even if the patches are small.

Wild Rooftops

Rooftops gardens can be much more than potted trees or tomato plants. Designed to withstand the weight and stress of soil heavy with water, the Vancouver Convention Centre boasts a 2.4-hectare (6-acre) living roof of native meadow plants. The roof is one link in a corridor of rewilded park habitats, and it makes a natural cafeteria for insects and birds.

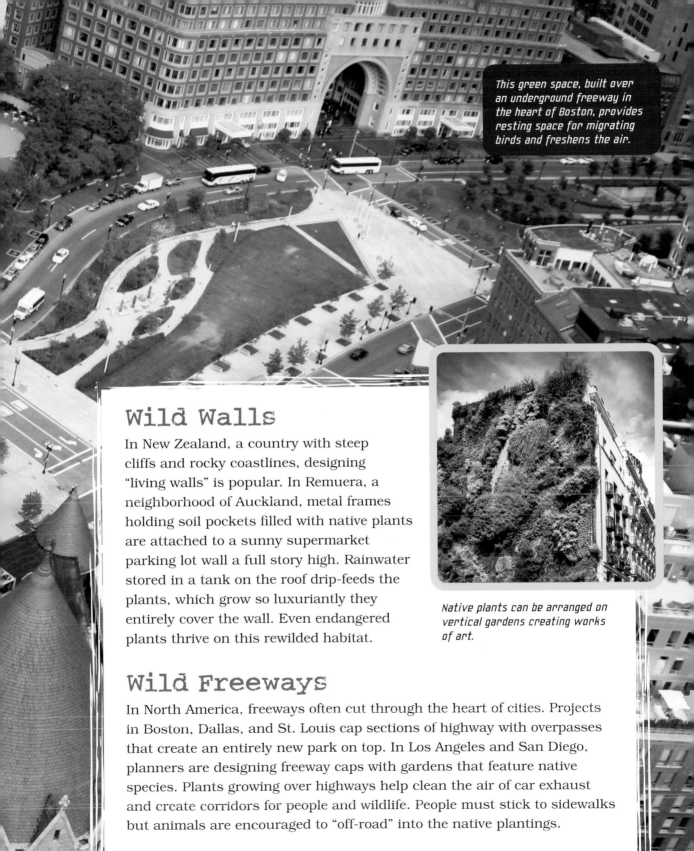

This green space, built over an underground freeway in the heart of Boston, provides resting space for migrating birds and freshens the air.

Native plants can be arranged on vertical gardens creating works of art.

Wild Walls

In New Zealand, a country with steep cliffs and rocky coastlines, designing "living walls" is popular. In Remuera, a neighborhood of Auckland, metal frames holding soil pockets filled with native plants are attached to a sunny supermarket parking lot wall a full story high. Rainwater stored in a tank on the roof drip-feeds the plants, which grow so luxuriantly they entirely cover the wall. Even endangered plants thrive on this rewilded habitat.

Wild Freeways

In North America, freeways often cut through the heart of cities. Projects in Boston, Dallas, and St. Louis cap sections of highway with overpasses that create an entirely new park on top. In Los Angeles and San Diego, planners are designing freeway caps with gardens that feature native species. Plants growing over highways help clean the air of car exhaust and create corridors for people and wildlife. People must stick to sidewalks but animals are encouraged to "off-road" into the native plantings.

High Park: Where There's Smoke, There's Fire!

Fire spreads under the trees in downtown Toronto, consuming dead leaves and flaring when it hits plant stalks and bushes. But people walking past show no alarm. Yesterday, neighbors were warned about the prescribed burn. Park officials keep the flames under control.

Every spring, people walk, bike, and drive past the controlled burn unalarmed.

A Prescription for Rewilding

A subway line, an expressway, and city neighborhoods border High Park's 160 hectares (400 acres). High Park boasts one of the last black oak savannas in Canada, a grasslands habitat with scattered trees that once covered large patches of north-central North America. In High Park, the trees grow well apart with prairie grasses and wildflowers beneath. The savanna depends on fire every 8 to 10 springs to clean up leaf litter so that sunlight can reach seeds on the soil. Black oak bark is fire-resistant, and a good blaze triggers a bumper crop of acorns.

In Toronto, fire rangers manage a controlled burn under High Park's magnificent black oaks.

For over a hundred years, fires were suppressed in High Park. Few young oaks took hold and now most of the trees are elderly. Without fire, the carpets of prairie wildflowers shrank too. Even the park's fabled wild blue lupine became so rare that the Karner blue—a butterfly that depends on it—disappeared altogether.

But the smell of smoke now wafts through the park each spring as officials burn a different small patch of the park. The savanna should recover with its prescription of fire.

High Park Rangers

Local kids sign up to help reintroduce and support High Park's native plants. The park hosts 41 rare plant species, 32 of which are found in the savanna.

In teams, the High Park Rangers remove buckthorn and other non–native shrubs that are edging out native plants.

In winter, Rangers make mucky balls of native prairie seeds, compost, and soil. They coat the seed balls in a protective clay shell and then toss them onto cleared ground. Come the spring rains, the clay dissolves and the seeds germinate with a nutritious start.

There are no plans for reintroducing large carnivores to High Park—coyotes and red foxes already live there. But the Rangers hope the rewilded lupine will attract the Karner blue again.

Lupine will grow through the ashes left by fire.

High Line: The Sky's the Limit

The lacewing larva swings its head and jerks its bristly body as it crawls along, caterpillar-like, hunting for prey. The larva will grasp its victim to inject saliva into its body—

Lacewing larva feeding on an aphid is a maxi predator of mini proportions.

dissolving the innards in 90 seconds—and then swallow the guts soup. No bigger than your little finger, this mini-monster is the right-sized predator for its small rewilded space.

In New York City, "greening" a street may mean widening one hole in a sidewalk around a tree trunk. No wonder residents came up with the idea of rewilding an abandoned raised railway spur instead of tearing it down. The High Line in west Manhattan may seem like a tiny attempt at rewilding, but locals love the spark of nature it has added to the neighborhood.

Living the High Life

The High Line is actually a railway trestle that, in places, cuts through buildings above street level. The trestle carried its last train in 1980. For the next 25 years, wild grasses, coneflower, smoke bush, sumac, and other hardy plants took hold. Because they obviously thrive in the habitat, those plants inspired planners. The new "rewilded" High Line, opened in 2008, is a 2.33-kilometer (1.5-mile) long pathway with cafés, art installations, craft stalls, and large gardens seeded from native species.

The only carnivores released onto the High Line have been helpful native insects like the green lacewing. Native insect pests have few natural predators, so every spring, teens are hired to hang cards covered with green lacewing eggs near known infestations of harmful bugs. Nearly two million eggs hatch into small larvae that frenzy-feed on pest beetles, moths, and aphids.

To demonstrate natural pest control to local kids, the teens collect both larvae and adult lacewings. And lacewings make for great nature storytelling.

The plantings have brought back native songbirds and butterflies long gone from Manhattan's concrete jungle. And teen workers have recently spotted falcons on the hunt for their returning prey.

Native plants grow through old train tracks on the High Line.

Wild Boars: Sharing Space in Berlin

"Lost! Family Cat. Orange Tabby named Oliver. Please call ..." You read the sign, taped to a pole, and study the photo. Haven't seen him? You'll keep an eye out and hope Oliver turns up.

In North America, if you live near coyotes, cougars, alligators, or polar bears, your pets can vanish. Tragically, sometimes a person is killed too. In Berlin, people share their city with a keystone species/eco-engineer that's determined to stay, despite the city closing in.

▼ *A mother wild boar jaywalks with her litter in Berlin, Germany.*

Wild Boar Zone

Berlin is proudly one of Europe's greenest cities. Wild boars have always lived in the surrounding forests, and they have adapted well to urban expansion. Resourceful and intelligent, boars forage in parks and suburbs. Digging with their tusks for grubs and insects, they aerate the ground, helpfully rooting out invasive plants such as bracken and brambles. They feed on acorns, fallen fruit, vegetable gardens, or carelessly stored garbage. With full bellies, they rest in empty playgrounds or snooze on roadside boulevards.

The tusks of male and female wild boars are dangerous weapons.

Berlin's 4,000 resident boars keep to themselves for the most part, but that doesn't mean they aren't dangerous. They will gore with their tusks or bite if cornered. And people and dogs have been injured or killed colliding with boars on city streets and expressways.

Opinion is divided. Some citizens approve of the boars and feed them illegally, others are patient and resigned to the dangers of living with wild creatures, and still others want the boars exterminated. Laws protect wild boars, but Berlin has a hunter whose job is to shoot troublesome boars that attack people. His work can be dangerous—particularly when boar-loving people attack him for doing his job. They feel it's unfair to blame boars when people have taken over their habitat. But how much risk is acceptable in order to keep a keystone species nearby? And what can people do to minimize the danger? Storing garbage properly and fencing their property are two steps that reduce both risk and danger.

Berlin's future rewilding plan needs to protect a core habitat for the boars as well as corridors to shield them from traffic and head-on encounters with people.

Garbage makes an easy meal for these piglet litterbugs.

Peregrine Falcons: From the Brink to the Ledge

Move over cheetah—the peregrine falcon is the fastest creature on Earth. They plunge after prey in a diving posture called a stoop, clocking at speeds twice as fast as a human skydiver. The peregrine deploys a baffle in its nose, which stops air from exploding its brain or lungs. And membranes lubricate and protect its eyes. Wherever they live, peregrine falcons are at the top of the food chain.

Poisoned from Top to Bottom

The peregrine's speed protects it from most predators, but the bird's biggest enemy is people. In the mid-1960s, an invisible killer—the pesticide DDT—nearly eliminated the peregrine. DDT was sprayed on crops to control insects. Smaller birds ate the insects, and then the peregrine ate the smaller birds. DDT caused the peregrine's eggshells to break, reducing the number of hatchlings by about 90 percent. In 1970, the peregrine falcon was declared an endangered species and DDT was banned, just in time for peregrine recovery.

Heavily used before 1970, DDT is no longer sprayed from crop-dusting airplanes in most countries.

In the United States, biologists bred peregrines in captivity and hand-fed them using adult peregrine puppets, so they would not imprint on humans. The hope was to release them back to their own habitat in the wild, but finding cliffside nests turned out to be too impractical. Instead, learning from history, they decided to release the peregrines on skyscrapers.

Back in 1936, a pair had nested on the Sun Life Building in Montreal— the first known pair of urban breeding peregrines. The falcons made headlines when the building needed repairs. The birds were in the way and the idea of shooting them was raised, but the falcons did a good job of keeping dangerous predators—in this case, humans—at bay, dive-bombing the workers who got too close. It was decided to let them make the building their home, until the fall migration.

When the puppet-raised falcons were old enough to rewild, the biologists released them onto the ledges of skyscrapers, where webcams recorded their progress. The falcons adapted to high-rise living, diving and feeding on pigeons and other city birds. Though the birds migrated south in the fall, some returned to breed on the same window ledges the following year.

Now no longer endangered, peregrines are still nesting on skyscrapers all over North America, with their progress live-streamed on the Internet. Birdwatchers also spot them nesting on man-made structures such as bridges, as well as on natural cliff sites.

Wild to Rewild: The Leopards of Mumbai

The drug wears off as the young leopard staggers to his feet. Where is he? Nothing looks or smells familiar. A jarring clang startles him and he runs. But this place is like a maze without an exit. He dashes onto a road and in between buildings, scatters a group of humans, and comes face-to-face with a snarling, bigger leopard. Finally, he bounds up the trunk of a tree and feels safe—for the moment.

Leopards, keystone carnivores, have always lived around Mumbai, India. Because of the elusive and solitary nature of leopards, there were once very few human–leopard confrontations. But as the city grew to over 20 million people, leopard habitat was narrowed to Sanjay Gandhi National Park (SGNP)—a wild space within the city. As the city's population became even more dense and crowded, suburbs surrounded the park's perimeter and illegal settlements sprang up in the park itself, putting people and leopards in close quarters. Today 35 leopards live in this urban forest, along with squatters and creatures, including wild dogs.

In the past, government workers trapped problem leopards and moved them to SGNP.

In recent years, much of the leopard's habitat throughout India was taken over by farms and expanding cities. This also caused the leopard's natural prey to disappear. When leopards turned to domestic livestock for food, conflict with humans increased, and a quick solution had to be found. Without considering all the consequences, Indian authorities decided to rewild "problem" leopards by releasing them into the SGNP with the others. Faced with unfamiliar territory and hostile local leopards, these stressed and starving refugee leopards foraged nearby, where the menu included garbage, pets, and sometimes a person.

The people at risk in the park are those living in poverty, without proper sanitation or housing. The government recently abandoned their catch-and-release program of problem leopards, recognizing this was a rewilding failure. Can India successfully rewild the leopard, and at the same time, improve the lives of their vulnerable, impoverished citizens?

Children collecting water are at risk when leopards prowl nearby.

Bermuda Balance: Restoring Night Herons

At sunset, the tapping starts. Each night, the red land crabs of Bermuda leave their burrows and forage for small creatures and tasty plants. The sound is muted at first but gets amplified on the limestone roof tiles; it soon explodes into a full-on clatter. Like an invading army, the crabs scale walls and swarm across roofs, snatching birds' eggs from nests and snaring insects, lizards, and anything in their path.

Bermuda, a small island paradise on the fringe of the Sargasso Sea, changed dramatically with the arrival of explorers in the 1500s and settlers in the 1600s. Newcomers took more than their fair share of the island's plentiful game. In addition, sailing ships left behind invasive species—feral cats, rats, insects, and plants—that decimated native species, causing massive local extinctions and knocking nature out of balance.

By the 1970s, Bermuda's main island was like one big sprawling suburb, crowded with people—both residents and tourists—and the super-surviving red land crab. Native but not wanted, the crabs took over once their natural predators were gone. Their large burrows erupted everywhere—in lawns, parks, golf courses, farmers' fields, and gardens.

Red land crabs offer little meat to people but are a good meal for a night heron.

Natural Pest Patrol

Local biologist David Wingate learned from fossils and local stories that night herons once inhabited Bermuda. He also knew that the night heron's favorite food is crab. Wingate coordinated the removal of yellow-crowned night heron hatchlings from a nonmigrating population in Florida. Rewilded into a nature reserve on Nonsuch Island, Bermuda, they were hand-fed bits of crab. Soon they learned to hunt for themselves.

Bermuda still faces environmental problems, but with a restored population of yellow-crowned night herons feasting on crabs, there is a better balance of nature. With fewer crabs, other species have a chance at survival. Nonsuch Island does more than protect the heron's core habitat. It gives sanctuary to Bermuda's most rare and endangered native creatures.

A night heron strikes its prey in the dark shallows at the water's edge.

Downtown Toronto: From Mine to Meadow and More

Squirrels scold as a girl and her dog descend into the valley. Embedded bits of brick secure their footing on the muddy trail. Their noses tingle with the pong of thawing earth, and the cool air vibrates with the trill of frogs. Blackbirds, robins, and a bossy duck chime together in a spring symphony. A hawk swoops overhead, nesting material dangling from his talons. Over six million people live in the Greater Toronto Area, but in the Don Valley Brick Works Park, all creatures can turn wild.

◄ Heavier than a coyote and browner than a wolf, a new hybrid species has come to town—the coywolf.

Mining Clay

For nearly a hundred years, the Don Valley Brick Works produced bricks used in the construction of landmark buildings in the heart of Toronto. When the clay ran out in the 1980s, the business closed, the site fell into disrepair, and the mining pit left an ugly gash on the landscape. But not for long. In the mid '90s, donations and a rewilding plan returned the quarry to nature.

Industry Converts to a Core

Diverting a nearby creek created ponds that refresh and filter water. Fish now dart in the shallows; turtles bask on fallen trees; amphibians and insects lay their eggs. Birds, safe from most predators, rest on floating islands.

Facing north, you'd hardly know this was recently an industrial site. This protected core connects neighboring ravines with pathways along the Don River watershed. A diverse ecosystem—wetlands, sheer cliffs, forest, and meadows—offers an urban home to coyotes, deer, skunks, hawks, and so on down the food web. A new hybrid species, coywolves—part coyote and part eastern wolf—has been sighted and may make Don Valley Brick Works Park its home.

Evergreen has transformed the Brick Works from a factory to a funky, multi-purpose venue.

At the south end of the park, Evergreen—a nonprofit organization dedicated to sustainable and livable cities—repurposed the industrial buildings and added new ones: a school, offices, a restaurant, and Toronto's biggest farmers' market.

Together with the parkland, this remarkable space—194 hectares (480 acres) in all—has caught the world's attention as a useful wild place, open to everyone.

Danger Zones: Nature's Comeback

Think about the damage that's done to Earth by the devastation of war, toxic pollution, radioactivity—no way the land will recover, right? Better to fence the area off with barbed wire and abandon hope.

People can abuse wild habitat in such a way that we worry the damage is permanent. The good news is that sometimes, as we've seen with the cod off the coast of Newfoundland, nature has a way of rewilding itself. But the result might not always be what we expect.

One Million Land Mines

In 1953, the Korean War ended with a 4-kilometer (2.5-mile) wide and 238–kilometer (148–mile) long "line" being drawn east to west across the peninsula. Bordered on both sides with barbed wire and guarded by two million soldiers, the demilitarized zone, or DMZ, is thick with land mines. North and South Korea are divided but still "at war," and no one has been inside the DMZ for over 60 years.

If it hadn't been for the land mines, this area could have been farmed or developed for industry. But today, the DMZ has self-rewilded to become a haven for endangered species and home to a diverse range of wildlife. Nearly 3,000 kinds of plants and animals live there, including the endangered red-crowned crane, Asiatic black bear, Amur goral, Amur leopard, and maybe even the rare keystone carnivore, the Siberian tiger.

The red-crowned crane has returned to the DMZ.

Pripyat is a ghost town lying within the Chernobyl Zone of Alienation.

Guard posts keep people, not wildlife, out of the Korean DMZ.

Lethal Radiation

In 1986, explosions and fires at the Chernobyl Nuclear Power Plant in Ukraine blasted radioactive particles into the air, severely contaminating a swath of Ukraine, Belarus, and Russia. Thirty-one workers died in the accident and thousands developed cancer afterwards.

People were evacuated from the site, and a "Zone of Alienation" 30 kilometers (19 miles) in all directions from the reactor still excludes everybody except scientists and special visitors in safety suits. Scientists say humans may not be able to live on the reactor site for 20,000 years.

Scientists expected that the radiation would result in a decline in the mammal population, but they were surprised to discover more wolves, badgers, owls, wild boars, and bears in the area than before the accident. It turns out that even though radiation is dangerous to animals, some human activities such as hunting, farming, forestry, and development are even more hazardous.

6 The Possible and the Impossible of Future Rewilding

Will the rewilding of a more suitable habitat offer a future for this mountain gorilla?

If arctic ice and snow melt, will the polar bear survive this century?

What is the future of wildness, and what role will we play in shaping it? Human activities so far have had a huge impact on Earth's climate, geology, and ecosystems. In fact, some people say we have entered a new epoch. The Pleistocene, or ice age, is long gone, and the Holocene, or modern epoch, may be over. Are we now in the Anthropocene, the epoch of the human being?

In our attempts to dominate nature, we have come close to destroying it. Climate scientists worry that in less than a hundred years, some species—starting with mountaintop species—won't survive in their natural habitats because temperatures will spike too high. Even if a few are rescued, there will be no suitable place cool enough to reintroduce them to the wild.

Conservationists have been trying to turn things around by using human influence in a constructive way to restore nature. After all, as humans, we are part of nature and depend on what it offers—clean air to breathe, fresh water to drink, good soil for growing food, and natural materials to build shelter.

Maybe rewilding is a promising strategy. But how far would we go to implement it? Would we give up ownership of all the land that rewilding requires? Can we live respectfully with dangerous wildlife? And how fully will we commit to turning back the clock? We can return existing species to the land, and with DNA technology, we can even attempt to create modern hybrid versions of ancient species. But what about trying to actually bring back species that were wild on Earth in prehistoric times? In short: How wild is *wild*?

Can DNA technology save the endangered Sumatran rhino?

Big Space, Big Time

What if you needed a home at least the size of 10 Walt Disney Worlds to survive? That would be 10 Magic Kingdoms, resorts and all—about 1,000 square kilometers (400 square miles).

That's the minimum home range one male grizzly bear seems to need. Cougars and wolverines roam through half that, but it's still big territory.

Thinking Big

Some scientists dream of a future when vast areas of continents are rewilded.

One plan calls for four "megalinkages" in North America—enormous protected core areas connected by privately owned corridor lands left green for conservation. That means persuading thousands of landowners not to develop their property. Impossible? For people who think big, "impossible" doesn't exist.

So much rewilded land would bring back large carnivores as well as smaller species, they argue. And the keystone carnivores would keep the whole system in balance. So much nature would clean the water and air, fertilize soils, and stabilize climate, all the while providing a beautiful, healthy home for people.

What has not been worked out yet is how people fit into megalinkages. Do we fence around the rewilded cores or fence huge enclosures where people want to live? Parents will never want small children walking to school where hungry grizzlies or cougars prowl!

The grizzly bear has the biggest home range of any North American land mammal.

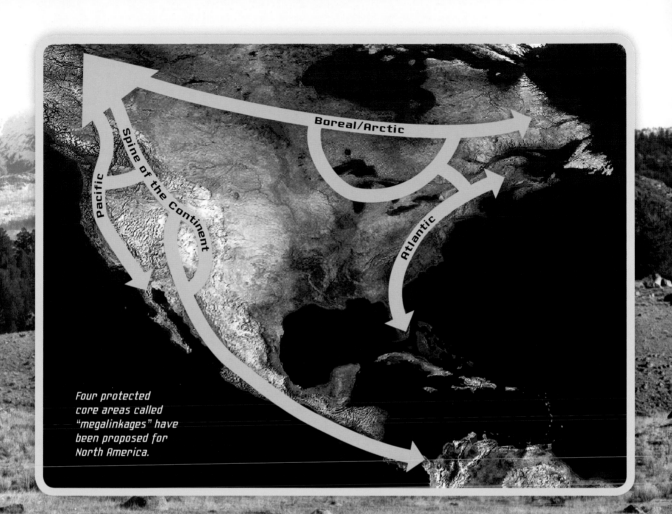

Boreal/Arctic

Pacific

Spine of the Continent

Atlantic

Four protected
core areas called
"megalinkages" have
been proposed for
North America.

Some rewilders imagine the day when cheetahs will chase prey in Alberta and Asian elephants will roam the iconic landscapes of Utah.

Time Warp

Future rewilding may recreate lost times. Some say we should rewild habitat back to when our grandparents were young. Others ask, why not rewild back to a time before Europeans migrated around the world?

Some scientists promote rewilding the North American West back to the end of the last ice age when American cheetahs and lions, camelops, mammoths, and giant tortoises roamed the plains. Present-day African cheetahs and lions, Bactrian camels, Asian elephants, and Bolson tortoises could be translocated from their own natural habitats to North America so they could stand in for their lost ancestors. These scientists propose a controlled trial in a large fenced area to see how the stand-ins would fare.

Can you imagine turning a corner to see an African cheetah chasing antelope in Alberta, Asian elephants drinking at a water hole in Utah, or Bactrian camels chomping on brush in Texas?

Critics of this plan—called Pleistocene or Ice Age rewilding—say we should spend our money rewilding habitat for species that live in western North America now. Why risk the unknown consequences to our grizzly and cougar populations, for example, by introducing creatures from another region or even continent just because they are distantly related to extinct Pleistocene creatures that once roamed the West? And would it even be possible to rewild back to past times now that the habitat is so drastically different? Would the foreign beasts thrive, or even survive?

De-extinction

You sprint past your friends as the trail winds through swaying meadow grasses. First you feel, and then hear, a strange rumbling, trumpeting sound. In your imagination, you picture a herd of woolly mammoths. What? Is that even possible?

Rewind. Scientists haven't cloned a mammoth—yet.

But they have decoded and mapped much of the DNA from Lyuba, a baby woolly mammoth found in the Siberian permafrost. And with new technology called CRISPR, they expect to slice some of her genes and splice them into Asian elephant DNA. Of course, they want to capture the long-hair and bulky-size genes. Only then can they try to create a hybrid mammoth embryo for a female Asian elephant to carry and then mother after birth. One Harvard scientist, George Church, predicts a hybrid baby mammoth will be born in a research facility within 10 years.

Why try to bring back the woolly mammoth? Dr. Church believes herds of these prehistoric eco-engineers—100,000 individuals—living in unpeopled parts of northern Siberia, Alaska, and Canada, would stomp, chew, and poop the tundra wastelands back into grassland steppes. He thinks that will protect the permafrost from melting and reduce global warming. Today, a private Pleistocene Park in Siberia already features species that have survived from ice age times, including modern musk oxen and reindeer. A small herd of woolly mammoth hybrids would fit right in!

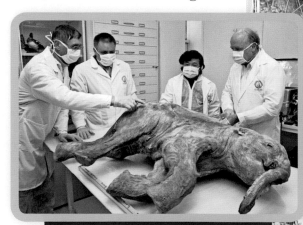

Lyuba, fresh from her permafrost tomb, is examined by Russian scientists.

Will woolly mammoth hybrids stomp through northern landscapes by 2050?

Some critics worry that de-extinction is an imaginary techno-fix that won't work on a large scale, and might not work at all. It could turn out to be a disastrous waste of money. Even using the word *de-extinction* might give people the crazy idea that we can severely harm nature—even cause species to go extinct—and then just fix it all later. Others point out that Asian elephants are already endangered—why not support them in mothering their own young? And when we cannot stop the illegal slaughter of elephants for their ivory tusks, how will we protect mammoths from poachers greedy for their ivory or a jumbo trophy?

Would this be fair to the human-made mammoths? Or to the wildlife that lives on the tundra today? Is the tundra a habitat that can ever be home again for mammoths? And what about the people who live on the tundra now and love it—they don't think of it as a "wasteland."

What do you think? Is de-extinction hacking or healing? Will the animals be fabulous or Frankensteinish?

Rewilding for a Better World

Rewilding is a bold experiment in environmental conservation that is teaching us more every step of the way. As we think about how to restore balance in our natural world by returning it to wildness, we discover how all aspects of our environment have to work together for everything to thrive. We need our keystone species, but they need a core that provides them with the right kind of habitat. And our cores can provide lots of wonderful habitat, but without corridors to travel safely through, everything from our big predators to the tiniest butterfly might not survive.

Kids lend a hand in conservation work on this stream.

We're also learning more about wildness. Does wildness have to mean putting everything back exactly the way it was before people came along? Or can wildness simply mean finding a habitat that will support a number of species in harmonious balance—even if it's on a high-rise, or over a busy highway, or far away from an animal's original birthplace?

And we're learning about ourselves as people. We are also part of nature and wildness. We not only have to think big to rewild but we also have to think deep. We have to take into account the consequences of our actions. We have to ask ourselves if what we plan is right, because we may cause suffering if we make the wrong choices.

We can't wave a magic wand to make rewilding happen, but if we keep thinking, learning, and trying hard, we will succeed. Making the world wilder benefits nature—and people too!

Volunteers help clean up
a coastline in Thailand.

Glossary

aerating: circulating air through something such as the soil on the bottom of a lake

Anthropocene: the name some scientists want to give Earth's present time period—or epoch—and which means "the age of the human being." Scientists argue that we are past the Holocene, or modern epoch, because human beings now essentially control nature, Earth's climate, and the environment on Earth.

biodiversity: the variety of plant and animal species in an environment

carnivore: an animal that feeds on the flesh or meat of other animals

climate change: the long-term change in the normal and expected weather conditions of a region—especially when referring to the change caused by a lasting increase in the average temperature. Also called *global warming.*

core: a stretch of land large enough to support all forms of life that exist there naturally in the wild

corridor: a route that connects cores so that wildlife can travel across built-up or unfriendly areas to find food or mates

de-extinction: the process of bringing back to life a species that has died out or gone extinct

eco-engineer or ecosystem engineer: a living animal, usually a herbivore, that creates, changes, or destroys a habitat as part of its normal behavior; see *keystone species*

ecosystem: a natural system formed by all its living and nonliving parts, including plants, animals, rocks, weather, soil, water, sunlight, etc.

eel-way: a ladder that gives eels a safe path around river dams

encroachment: the gradual taking over of an area not previously occupied, as when humans move into wild animal habitat

endangered: a species in danger of disappearing or becoming extinct

extinct: a species that has totally died out and can no longer be found in the wild or in captivity anywhere; see *local extinction*

fledge: develop feathers necessary for flying

food chain: a way of describing a natural community by lining up the animals in order of who eats whom. At the top of the food chain are the fiercest animals that eat other (usually) smaller animals who in turn eat smaller animals. Animals that eat plants are at the bottom of the food chain.

food web: a network of food chains in a natural community; see *food chain*

ground-truthing: confirming facts by actual field check

habitat: a place that naturally supports the life and growth of living plants and animals

herbivore: an animal that feeds on plants

Holocene: the name scientists give Earth's present time period or epoch

imprint: newborn birds and mammals rapidly learn to trust and identify with the faces of their food source, usually their parents' faces

incidental catch: unwanted fish and marine life snared by trawlers while dragging the ocean bottom for specific fish

invasive species: a non–native plant, animal, fungus, or bacteria that causes harm in a new habitat where it has no natural enemies and therefore can reproduce and spread unchecked

keystone species: a species on which other species largely depend or which helps to keep the shared habitat in balance. Categories include large carnivores, large herbivores, eco-engineers, and pollinators.

local extinction: what occurs when a species disappears from an area although it may exist elsewhere

megalinkage: a vast protected area that covers a large part of a continent

molting: shedding old feathers, hair, skin, or shell to allow for new growth

organism: an individual living thing such as an animal, plant, fungus, or bacteria

permafrost: permanently frozen ground under the topsoil layer that occurs mostly in polar regions

Pleistocene: the time period or epoch that began about 1.8 million years ago and ended with the melting of the glaciers at the end of the last ice age about 12,000 years ago

poaching: illegal hunting, capturing, or killing of wild animals

pollinator: an organism, usually an insect or a bird, that transfers pollen from the male parts of a flower to the female parts of the same or different flower and thereby fertilizes the female flower; see *keystone species*

rewilding: a large-scale conservation strategy that aims to restore and protect plants, animals, and their living habitats by setting aside core wilderness areas, assembling corridors to connect the cores, and reintroducing keystone species that have disappeared from the cores, especially carnivores. The word was coined by American conservation activist Dave Foreman and first printed in a news article in 1990. American conservation biologists Michael Soulé and Reed Noss first described "cores, corridors, and carnivores" as a base for rewilding in 1998.

Foreman further developed the idea in his 2004 book, *Rewilding North America*. Since then, most conservation biologists have broadened the "carnivore" category to "keystone species."

savanna: a grassland plain with scattered tree growth usually found in warmer regions

scavenger: an animal that feeds on dead animals or plants

species: a group of individuals—animal, plant, fungus, or bacteria—with common characteristics that can reproduce in nature

steppe: a large area of unforested grassland found in colder regions

sustainable number: the number of individuals needed for a healthy population

tundra: the vast treeless plains of the Arctic where the subsoil is permanently frozen

translocation: a strategy used in rewilding where species are relocated into wild habitat foreign to them but where they can play an important or keystone role

trophic cascade: a phenomenon that occurs when top predators have a positive effect on their whole habitat

waterfowl: swimming birds such as ducks, geese, and swans that are typically found in or near water

watershed: the land area in which the streams and rivers flow downhill in the same direction from a ridge of high land

web of life: a way of describing the complex interconnections between all living and nonliving parts of a habitat

wetlands: areas such as marshes, bogs, fens, muskeg, and bayous where water covers the soil some or all of the year

Selected Sources

Text

Donlan, C. Josh et al. "Pleistocene Rewilding: An Optimistic Agenda for Twenty-First Century Conservation." *The American Naturalist*, vol. 168, no. 5, 2006, pp. 660–681.

Foreman, Dave. *Rewilding North America: A Vision For Conservation in the 21st Century*. Washington: Island Press, 2004.

Fraser, Caroline. *Rewilding the World: Dispatches from the Conservation Revolution*. New York: Picador, 2010.

Hayward, Matt W., Michael Somers. *Reintroduction of Top-Order Predators*. Chichester, West Sussex, U.K.: Wiley-Blackwell, 2009.

Monibot, George. *Feral: Rewilding the Land, the Sea, and Human Life*. Toronto: Penguin Group, 2013.

MacKinnon, J.B. *The Once and Future World*. Toronto: Random House, 2013.

O'Connor, M.R. *Resurrection Science: Conservation, De-Extinction and the Precarious Future of Wild Things*. New York: St. Martin's Press, 2015.

Rabinowitz, Alan. *An Indominable Beast: The Remarkable Journey of the Jaguar*. Washington: Island Press, 2014.

Smith, Douglas W, Gary Ferguson. *Decade of the Wolf: Returning the Wild to Yellowstone*. Guilford, Connecticut: Lyons Press, 2016.

Weisman, Alen. *The World Without Us*. New York: St. Martin's Press, 2007.

Documentary

Fields, Ed, Dave Salmoni. "Living With Tigers." Discovery Channel, September 14, 2003.

Websites

Below are some specific URLs in the order the subjects appear in the book. These sites were active at the time of publication.

Rewilding Overview
www.cbc.ca/radio/ideas/rewilding-1.2914191 (image gallery and audio link)

Trumpeter Swans
www.pc.gc.ca/eng/pn-np/ab/elkisland/natcul/iii.aspx

www.trumpeterswancoalition.com/about-trumpeter-swans.html

www.allaboutbirds.org/guide/Trumpeter_Swan/lifehistory

animaldiversity.org/accounts/Cygnus_buccinator/

Prairie Dogs
rewilding.org/rewildit/prairie-dog-preservation-black-footed-ferret-viedo/

American Eels
www.dfo-mpo.gc.ca/species-especes/profiles-profils/eel-anguille-eng.html

Vancouver Island Marmot
marmots.org

Wolves
www.nationalgeographic.org/media/wolves-yellowstone/ and www.youtube.com/watch?v=KOONcUBjO8Q

www.lordsofnature.org

Namibia
www.worldwildlife.org/pages/namibia-the-greatest-wildlife-recovery-story-ever-told

Cod
www.heritage.nf.ca/articles/economy/moratorium.php

Wildlife Corridors
www.pc.gc.ca/eng/pn-np/ab/banff/plan/faune-wildlife/corridors.aspx

Monarch Butterflies
monarchjointventure.org

European Bison
www.rewildingeurope.com/news/third-bison-release-in-the-southern-carpathians-romania/

Oostvaardersplassen
www.newyorker.com/magazine/2012/12/24/recall-of-the-wild

Gondwana Link
www.greeningaustralia.org.au/project/gondwana-link

Jaguar Corridor
www.tbpa.net/page.php?ndx=65

Pandas
www.worldwildlife.org/media?species_id=giant-panda

The High Line
www.thehighline.org/about

Peregrine Falcon
www.natureconservancy.ca/en/what-we-do/resource-centre/featured-species/peregrine-falcon.html

Leopards
ngm.nationalgeographic.com/2015/12/leopards-moving-to-cities-text

Megalinkages
rewilding.org/rewildit/about-tri/

Wooly Mammoth
www.dailymail.co.uk/sciencetech/article-2634954/The-tragic-tale-Lyuba-Baby-mammoth-choked-death-mud-hole-42-000-years-ago.html

Pleistocene Rewilding
rewilding.org/rewildit/pleistocene-rewilding/

and www.huffingtonpost.com/entry/woolly-mammoth-crispr-climate_us_567313f8e4b0648fe302a45e?

www.monbiot.com/2013/05/27/a-manifesto-for-rewilding-the-world us_567313f8e4b0648fe302a45e?

www.monbiot.com/2013/05/27/a-manifesto-for-rewilding-the-world

Further Internet Research and Reading

Good keywords to use in searching for information on rewilding include *rewilding*, *restoration ecology*, *Pleistocene rewilding*, and *keystone species*. You can also include specific place names or species such as *Rocky Mountains*, *rewilding* or *African elephant*, *rewilding*.

Go to the site of your favorite wildlife, conservation, or naturalist organization such as WWF, Sierra Club, Nature Conservancy of Canada, National Wildlife Federation, National Geographic, and/or local Wildlife Trusts. Review the menu and type *rewilding* or your keywords in the search bar.

Image Credits

Cover and title page (wolf) © Prisma by Dukas Presseagentur GmbH / Alamy Stock Photo; **4**, top (swans) © MCarter / Shutterstock.com; middle (bee) © Kirill Demchenko / Shutterstock.com; bottom (lynx) © DSLR / Shutterstock.com; **5** top (sheep) © bgsmith / iStockphoto.com; bottom (beach cleanup) © rainyrf / iStockphoto.com.

SECTION 1: 6 (background city) © Frontpage / Shutterstock.com; bottom (deer) © jgolby / Shutterstock.com; top (traffic) © peeterv / Shutterstock.com; **7** (badger) © DamianKuzdak / iStockphoto.com; **8** (background, path) © karamysh / Shutterstock.com; inset (coyote) © Design Pics Inc / Alamy Stock Photo; **9** (fox) © AngelaLouwe / Shutterstock.com; **10** (background, tundra) © Vladimir Melnik / Shutterstock.com; inset (overpass) © Pics-xl / Shutterstock.com; **11** top (cougar) © Anan Kaewkhammul / Shutterstock.com; bottom (elephants) © Erwin Niemand / Shutterstock.com.

SECTION 2: 12 (background, wetland) © huyangshu / Shutterstock.com; top (buffalo) © westernphotographs / iStockphoto.com; bottom (leopard) © Stuart G Porter / Shutterstock.com; **13** (bee) © Kirill Demchenko / Shutterstock.com; **14** (background, ice) © FlyingMan / Shutterstock.com; top (swans) © MCarter / Shutterstock.com; bottom (poster) "Save Our Wildlife" by Dorothy Waugh. Promotional poster for the Department of the Interior, National Park Service, Library of Congress Prints and Photographs Division. LC-USZC4-8274; **15** (cygnets) © Lori Froeb / Shutterstock.com; **16** (background, etching) © Marzolino / Shutterstock.com; inset (prairie dog standing) © Martha Marks / Shutterstock.com; **17** (prairie dog and buffalo) © Danita Delimont / Alamy Stock Photo; **18** (background, eel closeup) © Rick & Nora Bowers / Alamy Stock Photo; inset (blue heron) © ejkrouse / iStockphoto.com; **19** (fisherman) © canadabrian / Alamy Stock Photo; **20** (background) © Pavliha / Shutterstock.com; **21** (marmot) © INTERFOTO / Alamy Stock photo; **22** (background, condor) © kojihirano / Shutterstock.com; **23** top (release) and bottom (marmot) © Jared Hobbs, Hobbs Photo Images Co.; **24** (background, lion) © mareandmare / Shutterstock.com; inset (gorilla) © GTS Productions / Shutterstock.com; **25** (oryx) © Nimit Virdi / Shutterstock.com; **26** bottom (tiger cub) © zilli / iStockphoto.com; (background) © Danita Delimont / Alamy Stock Photo; **27** inset (tiger on rock) Greatstock / Alamy Stock Photo.

SECTION 3: 28 (background, city) © wawri / Shutterstock.com; bottom inset (whale) © Seb c'est bien / Shutterstock.com; top inset (bicyclists) © Pavel L Photo and Video / Shutterstock.com; **29** (deer herd) © Christopher Seno / Shutterstock.com; **30** (background, wolf pack) © David Parsons / iStockphoto.com; bottom inset (three wolves) © Nagel Photography / Shutterstock.com; top inset (Red Riding Hood) © duncan1890 / iStockphoto.com; **31** (wolf howling) © Ronnie Howard / Shutterstock.com; **32** (background, wolf & buffalo) © thejack / iStockphoto.com; top inset (helicopter) © National Geographic Creative / Alamy Stock Photo; **33** (wolf eating) © JudiLen / iStockphoto.com; **34** (lions feeding) © Simone- / iStockphoto.com; (background) © Tiago_Fernandez / iStockphoto.com **35** (eco-tourists and springbok) © Jane Drake; **36** (background) © mladensky / iStockphoto.com; inset (Bruno) © REUTERS / Alamy Stock Photo; **37** (lynx) © DSLR / Shutterstock.com; **38** inset (underwater cod) © Poelzer Wolfgang / Alamy Stock Photo; **39** (background, historical photo) Paul-Émile Miot / Library and Archives Canada / PA-202293; top inset (fishermen) Photo by Chris Lund, Library and Archives Canada, K-1419A; **40** (background, horses) © Joost van Uffelen / Shutterstock.com; inset (greylag geese) © photonaj / iStockphoto.com; **41** top (red deer) © AlbyDeTweede / iStockphoto.com.

SECTION 4: 42 (background, Mt. Everest) © Yongyut Kumsri / Shutterstock.com; inset (Sri Lankan elephant) © vicspacewalker / iStockphoto.com; **43** (wildlife bridge) © Skyward Kick Productions / Shutterstock.com; **44** (background) © Lucilleb / iStockphoto.com; inset (bear) © bgsmith / iStockphoto.com; **45** (inset, sheep) © bgsmith / iStockphoto.com; **46** inset (Jerramungup students) © Amanda Keesing. Used with permission from Jerramungup District High School; (background) © GerhardSaueracker / iStockphoto.com; center (banksia) © iSKYDANCER / Shutterstock.com ; **47** inset (wallaby) © Auscape International Pty Ltd / Alamy Stock Photo; **48** (background) © Lynnya / Shutterstock.com; inset (single butterfly) © jps / Shutterstock.com; **49** (caterpillar) © CathyKeifer / iStockphoto.com; **50** inset (statue) © ppart / Shutterstock.com; (background) © AnnaOmelchenko / iStockphoto.com; **51** inset (jaguar) © Jamen Percy / Shutterstock.com; **52** (background) © Tamas-V / iStockphoto.com; inset (panda eating) © Onfokus / iStockphoto.com; **53** (baby panda) © dangdumrong / iStockphoto.com.

SECTION 5: 54 (urban deer, background) © DamianKuzdak / iStockphoto.com; inset left (Central Park, NYC) © f11photo / iStockphoto.com; inset top (fox) © Jamie_Hall / iStockphoto.com; **55** inset right (robin) © vktr / iStockphoto.com; **57** (background, greenway) © jenysarwar / iStockphoto.com; inset (wall garden) © ferrantraite / iStockphoto.com; **58** (background, burn) © Keivan Bakhoda / Alamy Stock Photo; **59** top (High Park burn) © Jane Drake; bottom (lupines) © DarZel / Shutterstock.com; **60** top (lacewing larvae) © corlaffra / Shutterstock.com; **61** (background, High Line) © pisaphotography / Shutterstock.com; top inset (rail tracks) © Albachiaraa / Shutterstock.com; **62** (background) © Florian Möllers; **63** top (boar tusks) © Neil Burton / Shutterstock.com; bottom (boars, garbage) Photo by Domski3, released into public domain. Originally accessed from Wikipedia; **64** inset (crop duster) © Photofusion Picture Library / Alamy Stock Photo; **65** (background) © hstiver / iStockphoto.com; **66** (background)© Steve Winter / Getty Images; **67** top (moving cage) © Sebastian D'Souza / Getty Images; bottom (girl) © gary yim / Shutterstock.com; **68** (background) © peeterv / iStockphoto.com; **69** top (crab) © riekephotos / Shutterstock.com; bottom (heron) © jo Crebbin / Shutterstock.com; **70** (background) © Jane Drake; inset (coywolf) © Tom Reichner / Shutterstock.com; **71** inset (Evergreen) © Rosemarie Stennull / Alamy Stock Photo; **72** bottom (red-crowned crane) Photo by Tokumi Ohsaka, released into public domain. Originally accessed from Wikipedia; **73** (background) © vichev_alex / Shutterstock.com; top inset (guard post) © vanbeets / iStockphoto.com.

SECTION 6: 74 (background, gorilla) © GUDKOV ANDREY / Shutterstock.com; inset top (polar bear) © Anette Holmberg / Shutterstock.com; **75** (Sumatran rhino) © mydeuter / iStockphoto.com; **76** (background) © VisualCommunications / iStockphoto.com; **77** inset (map background) © IndianSummer / Shutterstock.com. Details added by Pixel Hive Studio; **78** (background, pronghorn) © Jonathan Last / iStockphoto.com; (cheetah) © zokru / iStockphoto.com; **80** top (etching) © Morphart Creation / Shutterstock.com; bottom (scientists & preserved mammoth) © ITAR-TASS Photo Agency / Alamy Stock Photo; **81** (mammoth family) © Aunt_Spray / iStockphoto.com; **82** (background) © ferrantraite / iStockphoto.com; inset (stream cleanup) © omgimages / iStockphoto.com; **83** (beach cleanup) © rainyrf / iStockphoto.com.

Index